US

Published 2009 by Geddes & Grosset,
David Dale House, New Lanark, ML11 9DJ

Text by Gary Smailes

Illustrations by Planman Technologies

ISBN 978-1-84205-665-3

Printed and bound in India

Artwork references courtesy of and © Getty Images (10–11, 16–17, 25), Corbis (9, 22) and AP Photo (12–13, 15)

While we have made every effort to trace and credit the copyright holders of photographs used as inspiration for artwork in this book, the publisher would be glad to hear from any who may have been omitted

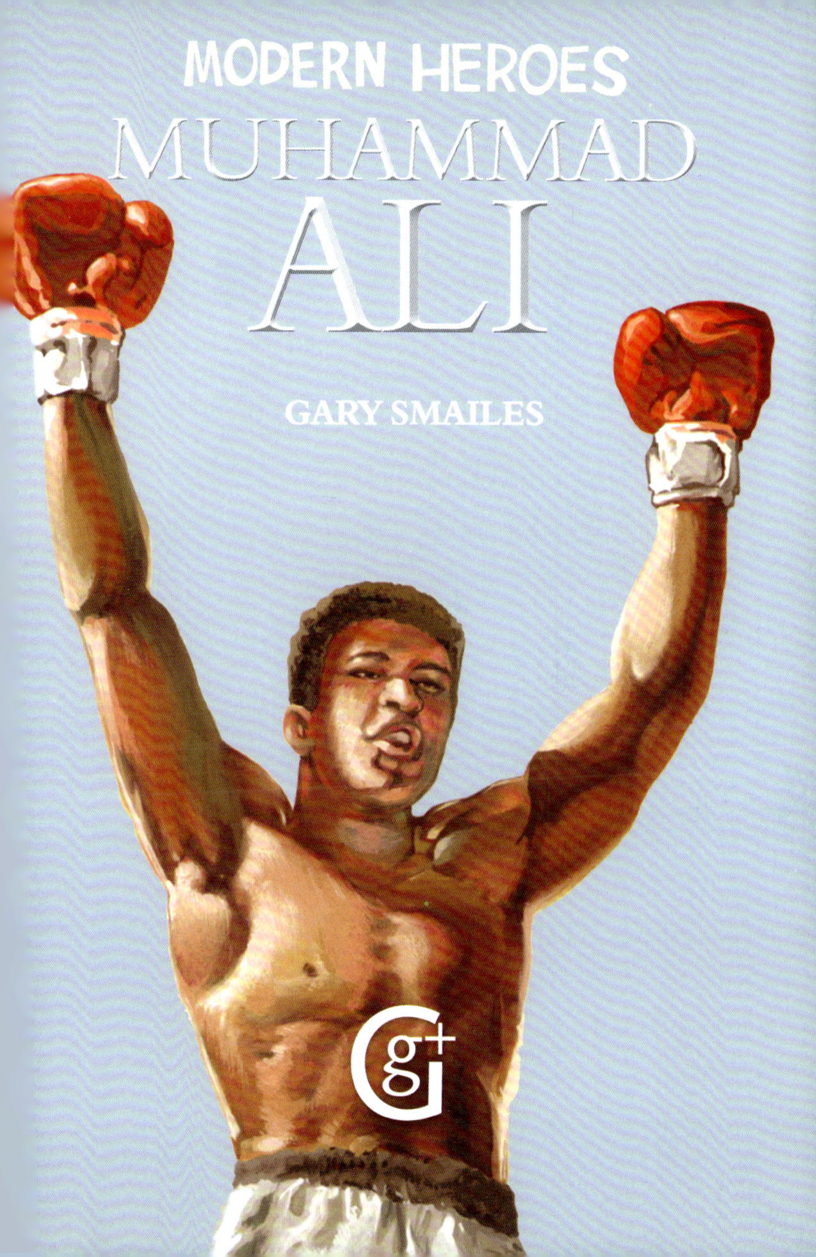
MODERN HEROES
MUHAMMAD
ALI
GARY SMAILES
g+

A Modern Hero

This is the story of a modern hero called Muhammad Ali – a black man who stood up for what he believed, no matter what the consequences.

Cassius Clay

Although we know him best as Muhammad Ali, our hero once had another name. First he was called Cassius Clay, but later – for a very good reason that you'll soon find out – he changed it. You'll notice that for one half of the book we refer to him as Clay and for the other half we call him Ali.

Cassius Clay was born in 1942 in Louisville, Kentucky, in the United States of America. He had a happy childhood, but didn't do very well at school.

When Clay was 12 his parents bought him a new bike. One day, while he was playing with his friends it was stolen. He was furious and went to see the local policeman. He told him that he was going to "beat up" the thief when he found him. The policeman suggested that he should learn how to fight first. Clay thought this was a great idea and decided to join his local boxing gym.

The Boxer

Cassius Clay had his first amateur fight after only six weeks of training. Amateur boxers do not get paid to fight. He won the fight, but only just. This didn't stop him telling everyone that one day he would be "the greatest of all time".

Clay was a natural boxer. He was brave, rarely got angry and was extremely fast. He would duck and weave around the ring, gloves held low, swinging his body to dodge incoming punches.

Young Clay trained relentlessly. He would get up very early every morning and then run a few miles, before going to the gym. All the hard work paid off. By the time he was 18, Cassius Clay had won 100 fights and only lost eight.

Boxing Training

A boxer's training routine might include the following: learning how to hit a heavy punch bag or speed bag, shadow boxing in front of a mirror, sit-ups, push-ups and pull-ups, skipping and jogging every day; as well as an occasional training fight inside the ring, known as "sparring".

An Olympic Medal

In 1960, Clay was chosen to fight for America in the Olympic Games, but there was a problem. The games were in Rome in Italy and he was scared of flying. So, to get over his fear, the boxer bought a parachute and wore it on the plane, all the way to Italy. In the light heavyweight division, Clay easily won a gold medal – he was amazing. He was very proud of the medal. He was so proud that he refused to take it off. He even slept wearing it.

He returned to a hero's welcome, but soon realised that some things never change. Louisville was a segregated town, which meant whites and blacks had to go to separate schools, and different shops and eat in their own restaurants. One day, when Clay went into a white shop for a drink they refused to serve him. He was black and it didn't matter to them how famous he was.

Segregation

Segregation means separation. Racial segregation means separation of the races. Several US states in the 1960s had laws that separated blacks and whites so that they had to go about their daily lives separately. There were many demonstrations and protests against these racist laws until they were all abolished.

US

"The Louisville Lip"

In October 1960, Cassius Clay became a professional boxer. He could now make money from his sport. He trained with a man called Angelo Dundee in Miami. Clay won his first five fights by technical knockout or TKO.

A Technical Knockout or TKO

In a boxing match, a technical knockout, or TKO, is awarded to a boxer when he causes a serious injury to his opponent. If the opponent is unable to rise from the canvas floor of the boxing ring because of this injury, after a count of 10, he is considered knocked out. A fight will end because of a technical knockout, and the boxer awarded the TKO is the winner.

Clay liked to boast and would tell his opponents just how easily he was going to beat them. The newspapers started to give him nicknames like "the Louisville Lip", "Gaseous Clay" and "Mighty Mouth". By the end of 1962, he had fought and won 16 professional fights. Many people now thought it was time for Clay to fight Sonny Liston – the world champion.

Henry Cooper

In June 1963, Clay travelled to London to fight Henry Cooper. Cooper was a big man, with a massive punch that they called "Henry's Hammer". The fight wasn't going too well for our hero. At the end of Round Four, Henry's Hammer caught Clay on the chin, knocking him to the ground. Before the referee could count to ten the bell went. Clay's head was still very groggy, but the fighter's team had an idea. They showed the referee that there was a small hole in Clay's glove

– how it got there was much argued about at the time. The referee ordered that a new glove was needed. By the time it arrived Clay had recovered. Clay went on to beat Cooper, but only just.

Spare gloves

There was much talk at the time that Clay's trainer had cut the glove. The British boxing newspaper ***Boxing News*** conducted an investigation into the "split glove" incident in 2003. They studied the original footage and concluded that Clay's trainer could be seen doing something with the glove while Clay sat dazed in his corner. While his team went to look for new gloves, Clay had extra time to recover from Henry Cooper's "hammer" blow. As a result of this, from that day on, boxers always have to have a spare pair of gloves at the ringside in case of such splits happening again.

At last the time had come for Clay to fight Sonny Liston. If he won he would become Heavyweight Champion of the World. However, just about everyone thought Clay would be beaten.

"Bear Hunting"

The battle took place on February 25, 1964, in Miami. Sonny Liston was a big man, with a very powerful punch. In fact, he hit people so hard that most fighters were knocked out in a couple of rounds. Clay was scared, but he didn't want Liston to know. He thought the best chance he had of winning would be to make Liston so angry that he lost his temper in the ring.

So in the weeks before the fight, Clay tried to annoy Liston as much as possible. He thought that Liston looked like a bear and started to tell everyone that he was going "bear hunting". This made Liston very angry.

Clay followed Liston around in his car, telling him he was going to "whup him good". He also set up camp on the front lawn of Liston's house, and then invited all the newspaper reporters to come and see. He told them that he would beat Liston in Round Eight, saying: "Round Eight, to prove I'm great".

At the weigh-in, on the day of the fight, Clay went crazy. He jumped around, shouting that he was the greatest and was going to beat Liston. Everyone thought he had gone mad. Clay was just pretending, trying to put Liston off.

Cassius Clay had a plan to win the fight. He knew Liston was not very fit, but he also knew Liston had a very powerful punch. Clay's plan was simple. He would jump and dodge around the ring for the first few rounds. Then, for the next couple, he would wear Liston out with lots of punches. Finally, when "the bear" was tired, he would finish him in Round Eight.

The Fight

When the bell for Round One went, Clay raced out of his corner. He ducked, dodged and danced around the ring. Every time Liston threw one of his mighty punches, Clay ducked out of the way. Not only did this make Liston tired, but it also made him very angry. Near the end of the round, Clay started throwing his own powerful punches. When the bell went, everyone was shocked that Clay had won the round.

The second and third rounds started the same way, with Cassius bouncing all around the ring. However, the two fighters soon settled down to a pretty even fight. The problem for Liston was that he was throwing lots of big punches, but hardly any were hitting Clay. This made him very tired.

By the end of Round Three, Liston realised he couldn't catch Clay, he was just too fast. Clay was starting to feel pain in his eyes. Some sort of substance

in his eyes felt like it was blinding him. Whether this was ointment from a cut under Liston's eye that had got on Liston's glove by accident, or whether it was something else is not known.

By the end of Round Four Clay was in agony. When the bell rang, he stumbled back to his corner, blind, panicking and ready to give up. Clay's team realised what had happened and covered his face with water. They told him his tears would wash the substance away, but it would take time.

Clay walked out slowly for the start of Round Five. He could hardly see a thing. Clay started to stagger around the ring, holding out his arms to try and keep Liston's powerful punches away. Each time one of the mighty blows came whistling in, Clay ducked and covered his face. If just one made contact it was all over. Clay struggled on. Then, suddenly he could see! His tears and sweat had cleared his eyes. He had survived Round Five!

As the bell went for the start of Round Six, Clay knew he could win. He sprung out of his corner and went to work on Liston. Now it was Clay's turn to be angry. The champion's face was cut under the eye and Clay started to land punch after punch onto "the big bear". Clay was amazed that the man could still stand up. He threw everything he had at the world champion. However, when the bell went for the end of the round, Liston was still standing.

As Clay sat on his chair, waiting for the next round, he wondered what else he could do. How could he beat the big man? Then, as he looked across he saw Liston spit out his mouth guard. The fight was over.

"Eat Your Words"

When Clay realised Liston had given up, he jumped from his seat and raced around the ring. However, at the moment of victory it wasn't Liston he was angry with, it was the newspapers. They had all said he would be beaten and he had shown them! Clay raced to the ropes and thrust his arms into the air. He leaned over and screamed at the journalists: "I am the King! I am the King! King of the World! Eat your words. Eat your words."

Clay was Champion of the World – he had caught his bear!

A Change of Name

For years, Cassius Clay had been a Muslim and a member of the Nation of Islam.

The Nation of Islam

The Nation of Islam (NOI) is a religious and political organisation founded in the United States in 1930. Those in the organisation worship Allah and believe that black and white people should live in America separately, but equally. The NOI aims to improve the spiritual, mental, social, and economic condition of the black men and women of America and the rest of the world. The organisation became famous in America in the late 1950s and early 1960s as a result of several things, including the rousing speeches about "Black Pride" from its spokesman Malcolm X and the controversy around its most famous member at the time, Muhammad Ali.

Ali pictured with Malcolm X

The Nation of Islam believes that black people should give up their slave name. In the time of slavery in America, the black slaves of white families took the surname of that family. Clay had inherited his name from a Kentucky farmer living in the 1800s. Farmer Clay had freed all of his slaves. Among those freed slaves were Cassius's ancestors. The Nation of Islam said Cassius Clay needed a new name, so he changed it to Muhammad Ali in March of 1964.

The Rematch

Even though Ali had beaten Sonny Liston fair and square, it was decided that they would fight again. The rematch took place on May 25, 1965, in the small town of Lewiston, Maine. The fight turned out to be one of the most legendary fights in boxing history. In Round One, the fighters bounced around the ring, no one wanting to throw any punches. At last, Liston sprang into action, lunging at Ali with four quick left jabs. They all hit Ali's gloves and arms. However, the power of the attack pushed our hero back onto the ropes. Then it happened. As fast as lightning, Ali swung a punch. It started low and flew up hitting Liston on the side of the head. The punch was so fast that most people in the crowd missed it. It became known as the "phantom punch".

Liston slumped to the floor and lay in the centre of the ring. Ali stood over the beaten man shouting for him to get up. Liston was unconscious for at least 20 seconds, but no count was given. Finally he staggered to his feet, but the referee stopped the fight. Ali had won.

Now Ali was the world heavyweight champion, anyone he decided to fight could win his title, but only if they could beat him. Muhammad Ali fought Liston in May 1965 – by the end of 1967 he had defended his title 12 times – winning all of the fights.

Vietnam

In 1967, America was at war with a country called Vietnam. During this time, if you were an American aged between 18 and 24, you could be drafted into the US Army. This meant that if you passed all of the army's tests you could be forced to fight in the war. However, even though Ali was 24, he had failed one of the tests and could not be drafted.

War in Vietnam

From 1946 to 1954 Vietnam fought for its independence from France. At the end of this war the country was split and the south was ruled by Vietnamese who had collaborated with the French, and the North was run by communists. In 1965 the US sent in troops with the aim of stopping the South Vietnamese government from collapsing. However, in 1975 Vietnam was reunified under communist control; in 1976 it became the Socialist Republic of Vietnam.

Then, the army changed the rules for new soldiers. They said that the low score Ali had received in the test was now good enough and Ali could be drafted. The problem was that as a Muslim, Ali didn't believe he should be forced to fight in what he saw as a Christian war.

The government was very angry with Ali and took away his boxing licence and his passport. This meant he could not box in America or anywhere else. However, they also did something worse – they took away his world title. Muhammad Ali was no longer the Champion of the World!

No Longer a Hero

In 1967 things looked really bad for our hero. He had refused to give up what he believed in, and as a result he was not allowed to box and was no longer the world champion.

Some people didn't like him simply because he was black. Some people didn't like him because he was a Muslim. Some people didn't like him just because they thought he had "a big mouth", and some people didn't like him because he refused to fight for America in Vietnam. However, what made matters worse was that some of his fans had also turned against him.

Our hero would not box again for over three years.

Return of the Hero

Ali had been friends with the assassinated black leaders, Martin Luther King and Malcolm X. While Ali was not allowed to box he was campaigning for African-American Civil Rights.

Civil Rights Movement

The African-American Civil Rights Movement was an organisation during the period from 1955 to 1968 that wanted to abolish all kinds of racial discrimination against African-Americans. They used non-violent resistance, such as protest marches, boycotts and sit-ins, to fight for their cause, but these protests were often met with violence from the white authorities.

By 1971 things had changed. The war in Vietnam was coming to an end and Ali had regained the support of his fans. At last Ali could fight again.

The Long Road

Ali's first big return fight was against Joe Frazier, a powerful boxer who, like Ali, had won an Olympic gold medal. Though blind in his left eye, Frazier was an awesome fighter and was world champion when he fought Ali. The fight was a disaster. In Round 15, Frazier landed a huge punch on our hero's chin, sending him dazed to the floor. Ali lost the fight – the first failure in his professional career.

Ali had missed his chance to be world champion and now had a long road back to getting another chance. He had been out of the ring for a long time and was older and slower. He needed a new way of fighting. However, Ali was not going to give up.

He now set about earning another shot at the title. Over the next three years he beat 13 boxers. At last he got another chance to fight Joe Frazier. Frazier was no longer world champion, but he was still strong. The fight lasted for the full 15 rounds, but Ali managed to win. Now he was ready to fight the current world champion – George Foreman.

The Rumble in the Jungle

George Foreman was a lot like Sonny Liston. He was big and strong, but slow in the ring. The fight took place in Zaire, Africa and became known as the "Rumble in the Jungle". In the weeks before the fight, Ali was back to his old tricks. He was loud-mouthed, calling Foreman "the Mummy" and always telling him just how he was going to beat him and win back his world title.

Ali had a plan to beat Foreman and he called it "Rope a Dope". Ali's plan was simple, he would let Foreman throw all the punches he wanted until he was so tired that Ali would just knock him over.

The fight started like any other. The two fighters rushed out and bounced around the ring, exchanging punches. Then, as the rounds went on, Ali started to introduce his plan, letting Foreman punch him. For five rounds, Ali took the punishment, but in the sixth round things started to change. Foreman's punches were slower and it was clear that the champion was tired. Ali saw his chance. He swung a high punch catching Foreman in the face and followed up with a flurry of strikes. Foreman was hurt. He stumbled and slipped to the canvas. The referee counted to 10 before Foreman could get up. At the age of 32, Ali was once again the Champion of the World.

A Thrilla in Manila

Ali might have been world champion, but one man would not leave him alone – Joe Frazier. For the third time, Ali and Frazier would fight each other, but this time it was Ali who was champion and Frazier the contender.

The fight took place on October 1, 1975 in the Philippines. It became known as the "Thrilla in Manila".

At first the fight went Ali's way, and for the opening rounds he bounced around, punishing Frazier with punch after punch. However, Frazier was strong and he soon came back. In the later rounds he traded blows with Ali, wearing him down with his strength.

The fight came to a climax in Round Eight. The two men stood toe to toe and simply rained a barrage of punches down on each other. After the fight Ali said it was "death. The closest thing to dying I know".

By Round 14 Ali had recovered and he began to get the upper hand, sending punch after punch into Frazier's face. Somehow Frazier stayed on his feet, but his face became so swollen that he could hardly see. Frazier returned to his seat when the bell for the end of the round sounded, but he never got up again. His trainer had stopped the fight. Ali had won what was probably the hardest fight of his life.

Retirement

Ali kept on fighting, even though he was growing old. In 1978, he lost his world title to Leon Spinks, only to amaze the world by winning it back a few months later. Ali announced his retirement from boxing in 1979, but he couldn't stay away from the ring. One year later, he returned to fight Larry Holmes, but lost in Round 11.

Illness

The fight against Larry Holmes had not gone well for Ali, but people started to suspect something more serious was wrong. Ali's speech had become slurred and he found it difficult to walk. Muhammad Ali was diagnosed with Parkinson's disease, which affects the brain and the nerves. It is at present impossible to cure.

Parkinson's Disease

Parkinson's disease is a disease of the central nervous system (that is, the brain and spinal cord) that affects a person's movements. It gets worse with time. Patients with Parkinson's have very shaky limbs, move more slowly than normal, have problems walking, and have problems talking. There is no known cause, though some people think that a severe blow to the head could in some cases be a possible cause.

Always a Champion

Although Parkinson's disease ended Ali's boxing career forever, he had secured his place in history by winning the world heavyweight title on three separate occasions over a span of 15 years. People will always remember our hero as one of the greatest boxers ever and as a charismatic man who fought against racism and spoke up for what he thought was right, no matter what the consequences.